A MAN'S INTEGRITY

*A study of
how men can
develop in Godly
character*

Jack Hayford

Publishers Since 1798

THOMAS NELSON PUBLISHERS
Nashville • Atlanta • London • Vancouver

ISBN 0-7852-7795-1

Printed in the United States of America

1 2 3 4 5 6 7 - 01 00 99 98 97 96 95

*This message was originally brought at
The Church On The Way.*

*It has since been edited and revised
for publication by Pastor Hayford,
in partnership with Pastor Bob Anderson,
Director of Pastoral Relations.*

TABLE OF CONTENTS

Chapter One:
Integrity of Heart—Preventative Against Confusion

As the shimmering waves of desert heat seemed to part momentarily, the mirage of a lake turned to a vision—no, the *actuality*—of a city. And there, in the distance, he saw the massive city gate of Gerar—one of the five power centers of the Philistine people.

Abraham estimated they would enter these gates in perhaps an hour, at which time his large camel caravan, populated with family and servants, would finally enjoy rest after the wearying 75-mile journey from Mamre through the Wilderness of Zin.

With his destination now in view, the man's mind became active. Political strategy was foremost in his thoughts. Though knowledge of this city was common— Gerar controlled an important caravan route between Egypt and Palestine— Abraham did not know its king well at all. It was this uncertainty about King Abimelech that most troubled him. He wasn't sure exactly how this king of Gerar would deal with him and his estate.

"I ought to be safe," Abraham calculated,

"but should remain on guard."

Having entered the city gates, Abraham soon halted his caravan before what appeared to be the main entrance of the palace. He considered for a moment how to best approach this unfamiliar and unpredictable ruler. Then his attention was seized by the swift approach of a small but official-looking man—Gath, the royal messenger.

Running towards Abraham and Sarah with frequent bowings to the ground, the sight of Gath caused Abraham to fear the worst; then, leaning over to Sarah's ear, he whispered something to which she nodded in agreement.

Smiling so broadly that it incited suspicion, Gath was finally close enough to speak, "My lord, your humble servant welcomes you to the glorious city of Gerar! King Abimelech wishes to find peace and favor in your sight!"

Abraham dismounted and bowed in response. "Your servant Abraham comes to you in peace and goodwill."

Gath bowed again, then turned his attention to the beautiful woman. "And may the wife of my servant dwell in peace."

"Ah," he hesitated but for a moment, "*this* woman? She is my sister." Abraham exchanged glances with Sarah. The reason for the earlier whispered remarks was now occasion for their agreed deception—"Say you're my sister, for the king might kill me to have you." It was a common understanding in this ancient world that an alien man with a beautiful wife was a "temporary citizen." Abraham, an outsider to this king's realm, was in need of great caution. Politically, this was a very touchy situation.

"Ah! Indeed!" Gath bowed again— smiling at Sarah in a new way. Then, quickly ordering his servants to bring water for the travelers, he abruptly excused himself and sprinted to the Palace entrance. Abraham's heart beat faster as he considered the possible meaning of the messenger's sudden exit.

Inside the palace, Gath burst through the doors with a rush—racing into the king's private chamber. Reflexively, King Abimelech whirled around with his sword in combat position ready to strike, causing Gath to throw up his arms in a moment of short-lived terror, "No, my lord! It is I, Gath!" The king relaxed his sword, but not his scowl.

"What is it!" Abimelech demanded— obviously irritated by the brash entry.

Gath cowered momentarily, then beckoned his king to the balcony with great excitement, "Come, my king, I pray thee—come, O my lord; look and behold. I have found my king the most beautiful woman ever to set foot in Gerar! If it pleases the king, I will bring her to you. Behold! Is she not the sister of Abraham our valiant guest?"

Abimelech looked down at the caravan lined up in the streets below. He squinted into the daylight and fixed his eyes on the woman seated at the head of the entourage. Even at this distance, her beauty spoke eloquently. It was the kind of beauty built from the bone.

Gath couldn't stop chuckling or nodding his head up and down. He would certainly be rewarded for this, he thought to himself as he glanced back and forth between the king's softening countenance and the prize discovery.

"Summon the woman," Abimelech said.

Gath vanished like a gazelle.

Rising up from a deep bow, Gath lifted his eyes up to Sarah while speaking to Abraham, tittering giddily between phrases, "Your handmaiden has found favor in the sight of my lord, the king. If it pleases my lord, King Abimelech offers many gifts in exchange for this fair handmaiden!"

Abraham briefly buried his eyes in his hands. "Egypt! This is Egypt all over again!" he silently murmured to himself. His thoughts flashed to that day twenty years ago, the last time he, through fear, had bartered this way, claiming his wife as his sister and laying at risk her chastity. It was an agreed ploy he had convinced her to use long ago.

On that occasion, Sarah had been summoned by Pharaoh to be his new possession, and Abraham's first embarrassment at such deception had been turned to deliverance by the grace of God. How could he be doing this again!?

Now, seeking to submerge his inner shame, he lifted his eyes from his hands to find Sarah staring right at him. There was a pause. Then Abraham tapped the camel's legs to kneel.

Sarah gave her husband her hand and dismounted. ("It is a natural and mature agreement," the man reasoned—forcing his mind to adapt some point to his defense. "And in reality, we are step-brother and sister." It was true—but Sarah's eyes and his own sense of shame could not be denied. There was no compensation by any line of reason for this peculiar behavior.) But all this flashed in a moment's glance between them. It was done, and now with a quick, "O God, help me," the plan was in motion.

Gath's greedy eyes stared at the dismounting woman excitedly, and almost babbling and chuckling intermittently and ceaselessly, he moved to take her hand.

Before leaving with the royal messenger, Sarah looked at Abraham one more time—a deep, penetrating look that, within its flash, held a lifetime of acquired meaning. As she did, Abraham was the first to look away, and with that, she had been surrendered to the king's messenger.

It was evening, and now King Abimelech was awaiting the arrival of this beautiful new woman. For hours, she had been being prepared with bath oils and spices by other members of Abimelech's harem. Soon she would be ready for entrance into the king's private chamber.

Finally, the doors opened, "My lord, the king!"

A valet escorted a magnificently beautiful woman through the doors into the royal bedroom quarters.

"She is called Sarah," he announced, then promptly left, closing the inner curtains and outer doors, leaving the two alone.

Sarah was hesitant as she looked around the room uncomfortably. The royal decoration of the bedroom was stunning, but certainly of little interest to the woman. Then her eyes turned to Abimelech.

The king tried to smile but found it awkward. He had never felt self-conscious in the presence of a woman before. Until now.

"Why?" he wondered to himself as he finished filling two cups with wine. The king motioned for Sarah to come closer, as he seated himself upon a mound of colorful silk pillows. And, as the woman drew nearer, he could smell the intoxicatingly sweet frankincense and myrrh perfumes wafting about her.

Sarah stood silent for several moments as the king held his gaze on the oil lamp he was igniting. Finally, Sarah sat down across from him on the soft pillows.

The moment was growing increasingly tense, and Abimelech began feeling somewhat impatient with himself. He was having difficulty even looking up from the lamp into her face at such close range. With an uneasiness that surprised him, the king finally forced his gaze upon the woman's large, dark eyes. Lit by the soft, warm lamplight, Sarah's beauty all the more hid her age.

The king searched for words. "So tell me of your people."

Sarah took a slow, deep breath and began to unfold the story of how God, Possessor of Heaven and Earth, called her people to a promised land. As she spoke, Abimelech wrestled with distraction.   It wasn't just her unusual countenance, it was her presence—or A PRESENCE. "Who IS this woman? Rather, Who—*what is this Presence I feel prohibiting my advances?*" Abimelech wondered silently. "Perhaps my recent loss of sleep has fogged my mind. Yes, that's it. Loss of sleep."

But as Sarah concluded her story, the king could only nod with a pretense of understanding, groping with her words about a God worshiped by her and her brother—the God called, "Possessor of Heaven and Earth."

Finding few words and feeling feebly out of control, his eyes slunk back to the lamp's now-dimming flame, the wick running dry of oil. He reflected silently, then sighed, and rising to his feet, he called to his servant. He strode to the window, his back turned to Sarah, who remained seated, wonderingly awaiting the outcome of the moment.

The servant entered, "Yes, my lord!"

The king continued looking out into the night. And without explanation simply commanded, "Escort the woman to her room."

"Yes, my lord."

* * * *

It was several minutes later—Abimelech

was crawling into his bed, shaking his head. He had expected to have great pleasure this evening with his newest acquisition. But for a reason he didn't comprehend, he had sent the woman away.

His thoughts drifted to the mysterious sheik who had freely given up the prize maiden in goodwill. "Abraham," he whispered to himself, lazily searching his memory as he drifted off into a sleepy haze.

Then it happened.

The Voice.

It was a roar, but ever so quiet. Cutting like a sword, but not hateful. Terrifying, but soothing. The Voice was more than words, it was the Voice of THAT Presence!

"Indeed you are a dead man," the Voice intoned. "The woman whom you have taken—she is a man's wife!"

Abimelech's nerves would have catapulted him out of his bed, but his muscles did nothing to respond—he lay frozen. He could hardly hear the words of his own reply to the Presence. With his heart pounding in his ears, he raised himself, leaning on his arms, and shouted in dismay: "Did he not say to me, 'She is my sister?' And she, even she herself said, 'He is my brother.' In the integrity of my heart and innocence of my hands I have done this!"

Silence. Then the answer:

"Yes, I know that you did this in the integrity of your heart. Therefore I also withheld you from sinning against Me; for I did not let you touch her.

"Now therefore, restore the man's wife; for he is a prophet, and he will pray for you and you shall live. But if you do not restore her, know that you shall surely die, you and all who are yours."

* * * *

It's a spell-binding story. And it's in this event, elaborated from the twentieth chapter of Genesis, that we have our first biblical use of the phrase *"integrity of heart."* Our imagination's rendering of the text is consistent with the historical events in Genesis 20:1-7, and as we conclude with the actual conversation between God and Abimelech, we touch the nerve endings of a mighty truth.

When Abimelech pleaded his case, insisting that "In the integrity of my heart and innocence of my hands I have done this," *God agreed with him!* "Yes, I know that you did this in the integrity of your own heart."

As confrontive as God was in addressing King Abimelech, the Lord *was NOT without abundant mercy toward him!* God knew that the pagan king was ignorant of the facts. He knew that Abimelech didn't know Sarah was really the wife of Abraham. And even though this pagan ruler did not have the same degree of revelation as God had given Abraham, he nonetheless displayed a fundamental reverence for God as Creator, which manifested in a consequent sense of duty. Integrity had been preserved in his heart. He was a man who acted upon that degree of integrity he *did* possess, and God honored his heart's intent. As a result of Abimelech's pursuing the wrong thing *ignorantly*, the fact he did so in *innocent* ignorance prompted God's mercy, who prevented him from stumbling into sin and its confusing aftermath.

But above all, standing as the towering, transferable truth which we today may learn, is the fascinating point in God's response, essentially saying: "I withheld you from sinning against Me because your heart was honest in your error; therefore, I did not let you touch her."

God didn't let him touch her!

We don't know exactly how He worked His first expression of mercy, but God sovereignly kept the king's hands off of Sarah! (Regardless of how God may actually have orchestrated such a prevention, Abimelech must have wondered why he just "couldn't get around" to enjoying this new addition to his harem!)

Further, in a second expression of mercy, the Lord warned him of his sin and of impending judgment. God gave him full revelation about the dangerous situation he was in and the punitive consequences that were about to unfold. Why did God go to such an effort in keeping Abimelech from the sin he was about to commit? What is different about this case than any other sinner's sinning? The difference is that here, *God saw the integrity of Abimelech's heart, even though he was misinformed.* And hereby, the first lesson the Bible teaches about "integrity of heart" is: *if a man's heart is honest with God, that integrity will help prevent him from stumbling into error and becoming trapped by sin.* In other words, God can find a "handle" in an honest heart, to turn it and keep it from its own confusion. It's a summons to learn to maintain such a heart of integrity.

But the inverse of this lesson is equally true. If my heart, sir—or yours—wills to have its own way, with an inner knowledge that our actions or words are in opposition to or in violation of a God-given inner sense of "right," God will abandon us to our own devices.

So, in introducing us to the power potential of maintaining our hearts' integrity, remember: fidelity to live in integrity begets a kind of "mechanism" built into the life; a preventative promise of God's readiness to intervene when we fall into situations of inexperience, unawareness, or unpreparedness. God will protect us—as long as our hearts are committed to a stance of integrity.

> *The steps of <u>a good man</u> are ordered by the Lord, and He delights in his way. <u>Though he fall</u>, he shall not be utterly cast down; for <u>the Lord upholds him</u> with His hand.*
>
> *Psalm 37:23-24*

As long as I walk in "the steps of a good man"—that is, as a man committed to heart-integrity, no matter how imperfect or weak I may be—the Lord will uphold me with His hand. He will be my Protector, Defender, Director, and Teacher.

It's time to start now, brother. What the past may record of failure can be forgiven through repentance and faith in the cleansing power of the Blood of Jesus Christ. Then, *beginning now*, irrespective of how little proven integrity or "honesty with God in your own heart" you may currently possess in your character, if you act on it, speak from it, and live by it from now on—God will give you abundantly more!

For if there is first a willing mind, it is accepted according to what one has, and not according to what he does not have.

2 Corinthians 8:12

Chapter Two:
The Integral Parts of "Integrity"

I was awakened that morning with a directive to speak on the subject "integrity." My one problem was that I didn't have a message on that theme prepared—in fact, I'd never brought a whole study on the idea. And so it was I was seated in the back seat of the car carrying me to my speaking assignment (just two hours away) frantically researching my biblical text and language resources for all the background on "integrity" which I could find. I'm happy to say, with praise to God for His grace, that I arrived with a sermon—in fact, one which the Spirit of God blessed wonderfully. But I also arrived with a bevy of brand new discoveries (at least for my part!) on the concepts undergirding this frequently used word.

Integrity is a powerful term! It is loaded with implications of honesty, trustworthiness, dependability, reliability and faithfulness, but what *exactly* does *integrity* mean—especially, "integrity of heart"?

Perhaps the best starting place is to look at cognate words (associated words) in our own English language, because the concepts there are remarkably illustrative of the precise meaning of the Hebrew word for "integrity," *thom.* In English, at least three key words virtually jump onto the chalkboard for analysis, all being clear relatives of "integrity": *integer, integral,* and *integration.*

Most of us were introduced to the word "integer" sometime early in our junior high math class. *Integer* is the word for a "whole number"; i.e., in contrast to fractions, integers are complete numbers—one, two, three, four—as opposed to one-third, three-tenths, or sixteen thirty-sevenths. This focuses the fact that when we are discussing integrity of heart and life, we are looking at *unfragmented—commitment, undivided attention, undiminished priority.* David was praying for this kind of heart when he called upon the Lord saying:

"Teach me Your way, O Lord; I will walk in Your truth; *unite my heart* to fear Your name" (Psalm 86:11, emphasis author's).

All of us know moments at which a quiet "ping," deep within the soul, has signaled a warning—an appeal that we *not* sacrifice a value, neglect an issue, surrender a moment, or violate an inner awareness of righteousness. But with uncanny ease, either you or I can silence that "ping" (which sometimes sounds like a giant "GONG!" trying to stop us) and plunge ahead unto the reducing of the *wholeness* in our inner heart.

For example, pressure of finance may argue that I fragment my tithe—reduce it to less than the biblical 10%. I may do this, but the compromise puts me outside the promise of God's blessing when my heart-felt, trusting obedience allows *Him* to compensate for tough economic hands by *His* hand of provision, not my calculated reduction. Or, I may leave a portion of the *whole* truth out of a conversation—refusing the "ping" which directs me to "come completely clean." Such moments of how we may fractionalize the heart's integrity are wrapped in the intended idea of *integer* as it relates to "integrity."

The Hebrew *thom* specifically means, "complete, whole." The Greek counterpart is in the idea of *eirene*, which is usually translated "peace." The essence of "peace," between parties for example, is that they are "one"; thus the picture of the *wholeness* in integrity. The heart at peace is the heart that keeps tuned and responsive to the "pings" mentioned above; the life that is *integrous* (i.e., is the one which is *completely* and *entirely* focused on God's Word, values, and will).

Of further help in grasping the meaning of "integrity" are the commonly used terms,

23

"integrate" or "integration." All of us immediately recognize the societal implications
of these terms: ethnic or racial groups are
brought together and interspersed as
one—as the *one* race of mankind, rather
than separated as competing "races" moti-
vated by competition or bigotry. The concept of "all together" is clearly present, and
when applied to your heart or mine, current
slang says it all: "Man, you need to get it all
together!!" Integrity means "I'm getting it
all together" on God's terms. Whether it's
how I use my time, serve my employer, love
my wife, care for my kids, keep my mind
occupied—whatever; instead of *dis-inte-
grating* under the fiery pressure of the
world-spirit, I am finding things "fitting
together"—integrating—in God's good order and way. It's a lifestyle summarized in
the words of an old gospel song, which
asked:

> "Is your *all* on the altar
> of sacrifice laid,
> Your (whole) heart does
> the Spirit control.
> You can only be blessed
> and have peace and sweet rest,
> When you yield Him
> your (whole) body and soul."

Integral is an interesting English cognate to *integrity*, which refers to "that which is essential or necessary to completeness." In demonstrating its application to our study, perhaps the most insight might be found by my relating the most exciting discovery I made that day I was desperately racing to prepare my message on "integrity."

As I was paging through my Hebrew resources, I suddenly was electrified to find the plural form of the Hebrew word *thom* had been left untranslated in most Bibles. In many places the word *thummim* simply appeared in exactly those letters. You probably recognize it, for any reader of the Old Testament has encountered the description of the breastplate of the High Priest of ancient Israel. Besides the jewel-bedecked chest-cloth which hung from his neck, with each magnificent stone representing one of Israel's twelve tribes, there is mention made of the presence of "the Urim and the Thummim" (Ex. 28:30; Lev. 8:8; et. al.).

The interesting thing about the Urim-and-Thummim, is that even though we are told *what* it was used for, we are not specifically introduced to *how* it was used.

The "What"

The Urim (meaning "lights") and the Thummim (meaning "perfections" or "completenesses") were "consulted" (see

Ezra 2:63). In short, when the people of the Lord needed a special sense of guidance or discernment, which only God could give, and human wisdom seemed undependable, they would have the High Priest inquire of the Lord "by the Urim and Thummim."

The "How"

While the scriptures only mention *that* this was done, *how* the priest did it is only known from reports which have been transmitted to us in the rabbinical writings. It is said that the High Priest would go into the Holy Place, past the Lampstand and Shewbread Table, and stand between the Altar of Incense and the Veil which separated this area from the Holy of Holies. And there—as near as he could move in drawing near to God on all but one day of the year—he would ask the Lord for Israel's directions from Him, and God would answer "by the Urim and Thummim."

Because the word "lights" is mentioned, some believe that a kind of "holy glow" shone, signaling God's will or pleasure, by some order of "yes" or "no" system. But there is a great practical truth in the fact the breastplate was over the heart and that the word "completeness" (*thummim*) was used. It would seem there was a combination of a supernatural signal, blended with an inner sense of God's peace, wholeness, composure, and assurance to the heart of the leader. And it is very instructive for us today.

You see, brother, while Jesus Himself is the only High Priest there is today—He's ours, Hallelujah!—there remains the fact that He has called and equipped us to be priests under His leadership (1 Pet. 2:5, 9; Rev. 1:6; 5:10). He has also given us "the breastplate of righteousness" (Eph. 6:14), which in a very real sense is a priceless gift of a heart-covering which will signal "right and wrong" to us—if we'll accept the signals!! The Bible says to us all: "Let the peace (*eirene*) of God rule in your hearts" (Col. 3:15).

Can you hear it! Just as the "lights and completenesses" were sensed by the ancient priests, so we are to live in the *light* of God's Word with the *peace* (complete integrity, wholeness) of God's Spirit assuring us when we are walking wisely, and correcting us when we are not. It's God's present-day "Urim and Thummim," provided by the ministry of the Holy Spirit who will open our understanding through the Scriptures and guard our heart through the comfort of His "completing" Presence. This is His "peace" *ruling in our hearts*!

That "peace" is not just a state of

tranquillity—not just a "feel good" on a sunny day when the sky is blue and clear. It's to guide us into all truth and truthfulness for daily living and decisions we need to make. If we allow the Lord, He will cause His "completenesses" or "perfections" to keep us from fragmenting our lives through compromise or folly—known or unintended.

I'll tell you, brother. There isn't a day that goes by that at some point I have to listen to that "internal umpire" saying, "That's out of bounds. Steer clear of that—go here instead." It's not so much an issue of my being tempted to do something stupid or to say a wicked thing, but rather it relates to and assists with issues of discernment and refinement. And it works wisdom in a life when the heart's integrity level is maintained through sensitivity and obedience.

But it's not without struggle. I'm sure that every person reading this has experienced the same temptation I have at one time or another, whether it is the Spirit of God or your own conscience speaking to you. You were warned, challenged, or corrected—and you closed your inner ear to that Voice. I fear I, too, have at times done this, for unfortunately that inner Voice of God's dealing with our hearts can be squelched.

There are many things that can cause us to become completely numb to the guidance of our conscience, to God's Voice, or to the wisdom that comes from abiding in integrity. The results of a numbed soul will too easily bring a fragmented heart which will entertain bitterness or unforgiveness, or worse yet, introduce spiritual blindness and deafness to the way and word of God's Spirit.

•   Only integrity of heart can guard against these blights on our soul.

•   Only integrity of heart will decide "even though this feels good right now, I'm going to submit to what I know is better!"

Maintaining our integrity by "complete and full-hearted" responses to the Holy Spirit's "still, small voice" will keep us instead in line with God's full, whole, perfect, complete, and entire will.

It's wise to beware concerning the relatively small things which will seek to invade this life of integrity. For example—being in a conversation where the quality of content takes a sharp dip below advisable integrity levels, and an internal Voice says, "Don't continue along that line of talk." There's enough fallen nature in any one of us to allow a short, minor transgression—"just a toe over the line." Maybe we're mid-sentence with something we suddenly sense we shouldn't be saying. But then, we think "it'd be too embarrassing to stop and say to those we're addressing, 'Hey, I shouldn't be saying this.' " It can seem awkward, or pretentiously pious, or—well, just plain make you "look dumb." Hey, I understand that feeling! And I've had to do that very thing.

Not long ago I was speaking with a brother on the phone and I blurted out something I shouldn't have said. It wasn't a lie, profane, or impure, but I had spoken something unworthy, careless, exaggerated. I stopped: "John," I said interrupting myself. "Wait a minute—I've got to go back.

"You know me well enough to know I'm not trying to appear to be some 'supersaint' or 'holy Joe,' but I shouldn't have said what I did a moment ago."

I went back, recited the comment to him, and then continued, "Just let me pray a minute, John." And I said:

"Jesus, please neutralize those careless words. Forgive me for sloppy speech and for in any way polluting my brother's ears with it. I put those words under Your Blood for covering, cleansing, and release. Thank you, Lord."

Then, I resumed. "Sorry, John, for interrupting—now, what were you saying?"

And that was it.

He knew where I was coming from, and we proceeded with our conversation with my integrity of heart repaired and intact.

Racing with God

Paramount to walking in integrity is to pursue our "race course" of faith in a *way* that does not disqualify us. The Apostle Paul uses two metaphors from the field of athletics—running and boxing. In both figures his objective is to point out the danger of "disqualification"—not of losing citizenship, not of death, not even of consuming dishonor—simply being "out of the running." The sacrifice of our heart's integrity can disqualify us from "running our race" faithfully with God.

Do you not know that those who run in a race all run, but one receives the prize? Run in such a way that you may obtain it. And everyone who competes for the prize is temperate in all things. Now they do it to obtain a perishable crown, but we for an imperishable crown. Therefore I run thus: not with uncertainty. Thus I fight: not as one who beats the air. But I discipline my body and bring it into subjection, lest, when I have preached to others, I myself should become disqualified.
1 Corinthians 9:24-27

31

Disqualified. That's a chilling term. It doesn't mean condemned to hell. But what does it mean?

I heard a pastor once describe this with a simple illustration. He said that in his desk he had many pens; but that one section in his drawer was for pens which no longer worked. They were no longer able to write or function properly, having been dulled or broken through misuse or uncleanness.

When asked why he kept these pens that didn't write, he noted they were either gifts from loved ones or commemorative pens from special events. Thus, he kept them as his—they were valuable to him even though they didn't write, but they had become "disqualified" for use.

So it is, God may not reject us from His family because we fall from His highest purposes through self-will or uncleanness. But the "disqualified" category can render us unfit for the Master's use, just by leaving us "laying in a drawer," instead of being fruitful, inscribing new words of life on the scroll of other human lives.

Listen! The Apostle Paul announces his own program of self-discipline: "I bring my body into subjection." The literal figure he uses employs the ancient Greek term for a boxer's knock-out punch. He is literally saying, "I deal my flesh a knock-out blow—putting it down for the full count of ten!" The reason? He wanted to be an instrument in the Master's hand—one who would win the match against the flesh and the devil. He determined to keep his heart tuned—to be integrated, all the pieces fitting together—walking in integrity.

Let's follow Paul as he followed Christ, doubtless in the spirit of David's words: "With my whole heart have I sought You; Oh, let me not wander from your command-ments!" (Psalm 119:10).

Chapter Three:
Integrity of Heart—
A Study in Contrasts

There are two unforgettable personalities in the Old Testament which provide a pointed insight into the meaning of "integrity of heart" when they are studied in contrast. They are David and Solomon—father and son: two dynamic kings who shaped the history of a nation, bringing it unto breadth of boundaries and unto beauty of regality.

From the time of David's early beginnings, God anointed him with success after success in battle. So it was by the time David's throne was established in Jerusalem, the boundaries of the twelve reunited tribes stretched over a vast domain which came as close to fulfilling Abraham's vision as at any time in Bible history.

It is in this setting that it seems David must have written the words in a song celebrating the power-potential of a heart of integrity. Listen:

Consider my enemies for they are many; and they hate me with a cruel hatred. Oh, keep my soul, and deliver me; let me not be ashamed for I put my trust in You. Let integrity and uprightness preserve me, for I wait for You.

*Redeem Israel, O God, out of all their
troubles! Psalm 25:19-22*

As you listen to this song, a heartcry is
sent forth to the Lord pointing out the
surrounding presence of enemies which
would seek to encroach upon David's
kingdom—to smite, to smash, to smother!
The king is painfully aware of a peculiar fact:
He has been blest with such broad boundaries, that there is no way he can secure
them with any number of troops. He is
vulnerable to the secret attack of an
enemy—unless. . .

"Oh God, keep me. . .deliver me. . .pre-
serve me."

Unless the Lord guards the boundaries,
there is no hope of detection—no early warning signals of an advancing host. And so
David makes an agreement with the Lord:
"Lord, let my integrity (the completeness of
my devotion to You) and uprightness (my
commitment to *do* right as You teach me
Your way—Lord, let those things become
my defense under Your hand!"

Do you understand, brother, what this
man is saying to God—what he is making as
the bond of His trust, dependence, and
covenant? David is saying, "Lord, YOU BE
MY DEFENSE!! I'll walk with a pure heart
before You, and let THAT be my means to

know that You'll keep me alert, prepared, and will direct me when I need to take action."

In short, David is pointing to a lifestyle that comes to terms with the fact, "I can't be everywhere, doing everything, all the time—trying to preserve my hindparts, trying to verify my worth; trying to win by the power of my scheme and hand.

"But, I *can* keep a right heart before the Lord, and let Him teach me, show me, lead me, and instruct me at any time, concerning anything where I need to take action that will keep the boundaries of blessing tended."

This isn't an argument for sloth or laziness, as though a pure heart doesn't need to pay attention to life's duties. But it is to note that, for example:

• I can't, as a businessman, "cover" every conversation of people who might try to oppose me or denigrate my work;

• I can't, as a parent, be everywhere my kids are and know every influence that's being brought to bear upon them;

• I can't, as a busy person in an informationally-exploding world, keep up with every new thing that might impact my well-being—either as a threat or as a blessing.

But I *can* do this: I can do my best at my

job, my family life, and my daily enterprise—but *then,* I need to be able to cast myself on the Lord's adequacy *in the knowledge I've not violated any trust with Him or others that would prohibit His free and powerful hand defending, providing for, and protecting me!* Like David, we can then say:

Vindicate me, O Lord, for I have walked in my integrity. I have also trusted in the Lord; I shall not slip.

Psalm 26:1

This is the David of whom the Lord spoke: "He's a man after My own heart!" And the heart of God was moved by the heart of a man committed to keep trust with Him. (It's another study, but even in David's most miserable failures—when heart-trust and integrity were grossly violated, we find his repentance pressing back into this heart-to-heart, close-walk with God [Psalm 51].)

Another King

Through the best and worst of times, God kept His covenant with David; David's boundaries were preserved, and his son Solomon inherited a broad and wealthy kingdom. Solomon was appropriately humble at the time he received this heritage:

Then Solomon stood before the altar of the Lord in the presence of all the assembly of Israel, and spread out his hands toward heaven; and he said: "Lord God of Israel, there is no God in heaven above or on earth below like You, who keep Your covenant and mercy with Your servants who walk before You with all their hearts. You have kept what You promised Your servant David my father; You have both spoken with Your mouth and fulfilled it with Your hand, as it is this day. Therefore, Lord God of Israel, now keep what You promised Your servant David my father, saying, 'You shall not fail to have a man sit before Me on the throne of Israel, only if your sons take heed to their way, that they walk before Me as you have walked before Me.' "

1 Kings 8:22-25

Solomon was saying, "Lord, keep this kingdom by the power of Your hand and promise." Only a few days later the Lord spoke to Solomon in answer:

And the Lord said to him: "I have heard your prayer and your supplication that you have made before Me; I have consecrated this house which you have built to put My name there forever, and My eyes and My heart will be there perpetually. Now if you walk before Me as your father David walked, in integrity of heart and in uprightness, to do according to all that I have commanded you, and if you keep My statutes and My judgments, then I will establish the throne of your kingdom over Israel forever, as I promised David your father, saying, 'You shall not fail to have a man on the throne of Israel.' But if you or your sons at all turn from following Me, and do not keep My commandments and My statutes which I have set before you, but go and serve other gods and worship them, then I will cut off Israel from the land which I have given them; and this house which I have consecrated for My name I will cast out of My sight. Israel will be a proverb and a byword among all peoples."

1 Kings 9:3-7

Here is God's answer: "I will perpetuate your kingdom, your boundaries, your family, your enterprise *if you will walk before Me in integrity of heart as your father David!!*" It's a clear pattern that holds promise for you and me: God will repeat protecting and providing acts He has shown in the past to those who walked with Him, but we enter into that covenant by moving on the same pathways of walking with Him as those who were so protected and provided for before.

This works in business, in your relationships, in your family, in your decisions, in your problems, in your opportunities, in your times of pain, in your high challenges, *in all your ways*!! BUT—it works *only* where a heart of integrity can be found at the center of a man's life and thoughts.

Solomon's Mistake

Solomon adopted a different strategy than his father David did for preserving his kingdom's boundaries. Instead of the pathway of trust (sealed with a heart of integrity), he took the pathway of treaties—sealed with the covenant of marriage to pagan princesses whom he married as a part of making alliances with neighboring nations.

But King Solomon loved many foreign women, as well as the daughter of Pharaoh: women of the Moabites, Ammonites, Edomites, Sidonians, and Hittites; from the nations of whom the Lord had said to the children of Israel, "You shall not intermarry with them, nor they with you. Surely they will turn away your hearts after their gods." Solomon clung to these in love.

1 Kings 11:1-2

This was not merely a matter of carnal passion. This is a man who is surrendering to "business savvy" instead of the "wisdom of God." It seemed wise to strike treaties, marry the neighboring kings' daughters, and thereby preserve the boundaries through the supposition that conceding to earthly wisdom would secure his throne. But it became his downfall.

"They turned away his heart," the Bible says; the same way that seemingly minor concessions of a man's personal integrity can do. While seeming insignificant at the moment—

- a slight indulgence,
- a "white" lie,
- a passing flirtation,
- a small compromise,
- an "adjusted" dollar figure,
- an unpaid-for stamp or office resource,
- a "fudged" expense report,
- an accepted "gift" for "special" services rendered—

The list of potential "princesses" welcomed to secure your own boundaries is endless.

Sir, Solomon didn't set out to have 1000 wives! He became the victim of a pathway that supposes that self-preservation and self-advancement are obtained by human manipulation. Instead, the Lord says:

OF PROTECTION: "Unless the Lord guards the city, the watchman stays awake in vain." (Psalm 127:1)

OF PROMOTION: "Promotion comes neither from the east, west, or south. . .for God puts down one and exalts another." (Psalm 75:6, 7)

The perpetuation of God's purposes in our lives is assured on the grounds of our simple, childlike openness and obedience to Him. Integrity of heart is *not* attained through a legalistic attention to ritual law. Integrity of heart is *not* the result of having mastered eerie spiritual discipline. But integrity of heart IS the result of a man who will (1) keep tuned to the "pings" of Holy Spirit correction prompting his soul, and who will (2) keep wholly, completely, entirely dependent upon the Lord.

Little children, keep yourselves from idols. 1 John 5:21

Keep your heart with all diligence, for out of it spring the issues of life.
Proverbs 4:23

Chapter Four:
Men Learning Integrity in the Business Place

Some of the most dynamic insights we ever gain come straight from the experience of others who tell of their learning, however imperfectly, to apply God's Word to the practical details of their lives. I've invited nine men from among the hundreds I've watched grow into men of integrity, to briefly relate tension points which became triumph points. These faced very real "integrity" issues, and each in different circumstances overcame an assortment of obstacles that would have rendered them "disqualified," had they not applied biblical principles.

Sensitivity to these brothers, who have been willing to share their weaknesses and strengths with us, recommends that I refer to them by profession only. The testimonies are theirs. They are true. And the integrity issues dealt with in realms of business, morality, relationships, and spiritual leadership will, I hope, inspire you just as those brothers have inspired me.

The Business Deal
An investment real estate broker with a large Los Angeles firm.

It was the first week of 1990. I would

later call this season the "financial winter of my life." There was no fruit, no leaves, no indication of anything particularly good about to "bud" forth in our lives financially speaking. Things looked bleak, but we stood fast waiting for the blessing of the Lord.

Then a very large deal came into the works. It was a $5 million sale that promised to yield a *huge* commission! Needless to say, this was an exciting prospect.

But suddenly the heart-rending news came. It was discovered that the buyer was engaged in a "double escrow," which meant that although he was buying it at $5 million, he was turning around to sell it at $7 million to a controlled buyer with a "rigged" appraisal. What he was doing was dishonest, and I knew I couldn't participate in this scam. So, I handed the sale over to another broker, refusing to handle the deal—and knowing I was giving away an easy-money windfall.

That was tough. For it was a *lot* of money.

Two years later at our church, the Holy Spirit had declared the New Year to be "The Year of the Lord's Redeemed." My wife and I reached back in faith and prayed that God would redeem that large sale that went bad at the last minute. Because we had acted *in the integrity of our hearts*, we believed that the Lord would repay us.

There were a number of business deals that surfaced throughout the year which looked like they might be God's "redemption" of that horrible disappointment two years before, but each one of them, for one reason or another, fell through.

On December 21st—nearly the last week of "The Year of the Lord's Redeemed"—as I was leaving with my family for a Christmas trip, the phone rang. It was a bank who owned a large property upon which, earlier that year, one of my clients had made an offer. But his offer had been declined in favor of a higher offer made by someone else. Now the caller apprised me that that higher offer had fallen out of escrow, and as a result, this was a "panic" call from the bank, which needed to sell the property before the year ended. My client's offer of $5.2 million was accepted, and precisely on December 31st—the last day of the "Year of the Lord's Redeemed"—the escrow closed. The commission it yielded was the largest I've ever had the pleasure of receiving—and all the more gratifying for it was received with a *free* heart, unencumbered by anything less than a fullness of integrity.

A Subtle Issue of Discrimination

A *vice-president for a major financial institution who manages a portfolio of real estate investments for pension fund clients.*

For many years I've subscribed to the belief that the "good" and the "right" courses of action in business are the same—whether I'm dealing with believers or non-believers. Unfortunately, with disturbing frequency, I have experienced a problem when dealing with other Christians who didn't grasp or apply this principle. It seems that once they found out I was also a believer, they would expect me to give them special concessions or render to them preferential treatment just because they were believers. While I often enjoyed business-related fellowship with other Christians, it seemed to me that *right* dealings were *right*, no matter what the other party believed in terms of their spiritual commitment. Why should I treat a Christian with "more fairness" and a non-believer with less? Without my consciously realizing it, these experiences with other Christians made me progressively reluctant to openly proclaim my faith to other believers whom I might encounter in the course of my business. But with time, the Lord began to deal with me about this issue.

Several years ago I had a group of commercial properties in Texas added to my portfolio, including a notable shopping center in Austin—a property which was in serious trouble. My first order of business was to select and hire a local real estate broker to assist me in leasing the property, preferably one with a reputation for being the "best in town." During my first couple of trips there I talked with as many people in the business as I could, gathering referrals for my file. Interestingly enough, the name of one particular broker kept coming up with notable frequency. Jill had a reputation for high integrity and great effectiveness in her work. So I arranged a meeting with Jill, and in the course of casual conversation, we discovered that we were both Christians.

At first, I was tempted not to hire Jill. I was afraid that someone might accuse me of favoring her because she was a believer (and an outspoken one, at that). And I was concerned that I might have the same problem with her that I'd so often had with other Christians in the business—that she would expect me to somehow give her firm some special allowances because of our mutual faith in Christ. However, I realized that since I'd made up my mind to hire Jill *before* I knew she was a believer, to *not* hire her now would mean I'd be making a decision based solely on her Christianity—a violation of my own heart integrity. I would be doing the very same thing I had felt so strongly against—the very thing I didn't want people to do to me: act differently towards me because I was a Christian. And so I made my decision. I engaged Jill to be my Austin broker.

Over the ensuing three years, God both blessed our business enterprise and expanded my personal experience with Kingdom power at work in the business place. I'd never before prayed with a business-partner to accomplish specific business objectives. A little more than a year after praying together that God would help us lease the project's anchor tenant space (vacant for five years), Jill and I stood in the exact same place where we had prayed—only now we gazed not at a vacant space, but at the grand opening of the project's new anchor department store!

In another situation, our decision to lean on the generous side in calculating another broker's commission rights ultimately resulted in Jill leading that broker to the Lord.

Through these experiences I have learned a rich lesson not to be an "undercover" Christian in the workplace! The genuine exercise of Kingdom principles and the dynamics of agreement in prayer with other Christians has made for broader horizons of triumph in my business world—much more than I ever expected it would.

Taking An Offensive Stance

An international business consultant specializing in information systems architecture for Fortune 500 companies and mega-corporations.

It never goes away. The Lord deals with me all the time about issues of integrity. It's not because I'm weak or lukewarm in my commitment to Jesus. But the opportunities to compromise are ever-present. This is accentuated by the fact that as an international consultant, I'm traveling about 40% of the time. During many weeks of the year I'm away from home four days out of seven. I know from personal experience that business trips can be tough on Christians!

But the Lord has taught me how to approach this difficult way of life: I've learned how to put temptation on the *defensive*.

I no longer turn on the TV while in a hotel room. When I check into a hotel room I lay hands on the bed, the walls, the doors, and the windows, and I engage in spiritual warfare. I bind up any negative spiritual influences that may be present in that room. I pray against any spiritual residue that may be left over from sin that could have been committed in that room—spiritual influences that would seek to creep into my life. Another important part of my spiritual arsenal, especially in hotel rooms, is worship and praise to the Lord.

As a guest speaker on the road, I also go down to the large hotel conference rooms long before people arrive and I pray over the seats, over the podium—and in short, I storm the gates of heaven seeking God's Kingdom to come and be established in that place. I ask that God's will would be done on earth—in the arena of my business dealings—as it is in Heaven. I seek the Lordship of Jesus to rule in my sphere of influence.

I realize this may sound radical to you, but I assure you, I'm *not* a religious zealot! I simply love the Lord. And this kind of spiritual offensive not only keeps my integrity in check—at every level—but it has spiritual impact on others. It influences people who don't even know the Lord because they are being prayed for diligently.

As men living in the age of super computers, stock market realities, and marketing issues—whatever our line of work may be—we *have* to come to grips with issues of the invisible spiritual realm and how they affect our integrity.

For we do not wrestle against flesh and blood, but against principalities, against powers, against the rulers of the darkness of this age, against spiritual hosts of wickedness in the heavenly places.
Ephesians 6:12

Our human frailty must constantly face spiritual forces of temptation that seek to undo us. If we don't take an aggressive stand against issues of compromise, and pursue the Lord diligently in places where we might stumble, then our chances for success will be dramatically limited.

With the consequences of moral failure being so great, we are wise to keep temptation on the defensive. Try it. Go on the *offensive* against sin. It works—and victory *can* be realized!!

Chapter Five:
Men Learning Integrity in the Face of Moral Temptation

Having a "Single" Eye

Logistics Manager who has worked on NASA's Space Shuttle program. He's been married for over 30 years.

How many of you are TV channel flickers? By that I mean a person who is constantly changing channels with a TV remote so you can watch bits of many programs almost simultaneously. To the chagrin of my wife, I must plead guilty to this practice, but never did I imagine that this would have such a negative impact on my role as priest of my home. Let me explain what happened.

Recently, my wife and I subscribed to a basic cable system with some 72 channels to flick through ("hog heaven" for a bonafide "flicker"). We didn't want any of the premium channels or the decoder box that comes with them. That way, when you flick through unwanted channels the image appears as a series of wavy lines that makes it unviewable. That's what we understood, anyway.

One night, while flicking my way through TV land, I came across one of the premium channels. For some reason, the wavy lines were minimal and I could see clearly what was going on: men and women engaged in sex. I was surprised and shocked at what was on the screen. Even so, I allowed 20-30 seconds of observation to pass—feeling upset and disgusted at such garbage— nevertheless, I watched. I finally turned it off. There was a "yucky" feeling in my spirit for I knew I had done wrong by letting that junk enter the lamp of my soul, even though it was only a half a minute. I should have repented right then and there, but I didn't. I just shrugged it off and vowed to myself not to do that anymore. I didn't think much more about it, nor did I tell my wife what happened.

That night at 2:30 a.m. my wife and I were abruptly awakened by the ring of the phone. Since the phone is on my wife's side of the bed, she answered it. On the other end of the line was an obscene caller, whom my wife interrupted with words something like, "God loves you and He has a much better plan for your life than this kind of stuff," and she hung up the phone.

While all this was going on, the Lord was speaking to me. *So very clearly* He was telling me that what I had done had "uncovered" our home. I was responsible for letting that evil—in the form of a perverted phone call—come into my house and into my wife's ears. Because of what I allowed my eyes to see, I had, by my actions, "given permission" to the hosts of spiritual darkness to invade my dwelling—to arrange that call. My heart sank at the reality of knowing how true that was. I groaned at the thought of disappointing the Lord. Right then—after repenting before the Lord and confessing my sin to my wife—I settled the matter. And we went back to sleep. But what a vivid lesson.

I learned that my maintaining purity and integrity before the Lord will affect everything in my family's lives. Walking purely will prevent the enemy from having any inroads through which he can attack my family or me. I was reminded that as priest of my home, I needed to let my mind dwell on the words of Philippians 4:8, which urges us about monitoring our minds:

Finally, brethren, whatever things are true, whatever things are noble, whatever things are just, whatever things are pure, whatever things are lovely, whatever things are of good report, if there is any virtue and if there is anything praiseworthy; meditate on these things.

Wrestling with Pornography

A former student who now serves on a church staff.

My introduction to pornography was as a little boy. My friend's father had a whole collection of pornographic magazines which I had the opportunity to look through on a couple of occasions.

That was the starting point of my many years of bondage to pornography. I would sneak peeks at the girlie magazines in drug stores and would get my hands on them whenever I got the chance.

Over the years, that escalated to hard-core magazines and X-rated movies. I could never seem to get enough of it. I really loved looking at that stuff.

There was one thing that made this part of my life rather difficult. I was a Christian, and had been for several years, but I found I had become *"blinded"* by my constant staring at pornographic material. Eventually, however, through involvement with men's gatherings at our church, I began to break through the blindness—I began feeling true guilt over looking at the pornography, and with the beginnings of these convictions, the wrestling match began.

I would weep before the Lord for my sense of shame and helplessness. I would stand on the Word of God and declare, "No temptation has overtaken you except such as is common to man; but God is faithful, who will not allow you to be tempted beyond what you are able, but with the temptation will also make the way of escape, that you may be able to bear it" (1 Cor. 10:13). I would quote Romans 6:14, "For sin shall not have dominion over you . . ."

I don't mean to (nor do I) minimize the power of the Word of God. And I don't mean to make light the power potential in speaking God's Word into situations that you face. But it wasn't making the difference in my life. I would go through seasons of victory where I would not yield to temptation, or feel very tempted. In my early 20's I even went more than two years without looking at pornography. But self-sufficiency—trusting in my own strength—was about to catch up with me.

One day, opening a magazine, I opened the door "just a crack." But to my embarrassment, I got "bashed in the head" as I began stumbling again. It was not with the same frequency as in the past, but it was enough to keep me feeling guilty and feeling like a hypocrite. Why? Because here I was, "Mr. Mature Christian"—having been a Christian more than half my life, and now even working in a church, and *still* not walking in the victory of a Christ-filled life in the Spirit.

But a new day dawned. And I began to experience a new level of deliverance as I began to OBEY the scripture in James 5:16:

> *Confess your trespasses to one another, and pray for one another, that you may be healed. The effective, fervent prayer of a righteous man avails much.*

It took a great deal of humbling myself to open up to someone else, and to—with integrity of heart—share the "crud" that was in my life. But I knew if I obeyed God and went beyond my own feelings, He would meet me there and do the work in me that needed to be done. And He has, PRAISE GOD!

As long as I kept the sin only "between God and me," I could not gain the victory.

I knew I was forgiven.

I knew I had been cleansed by the precious Blood of Jesus.

But as long as nobody else knew about it, it was easy to sin again. While I didn't *plot* to keep on sinning, it seemed I couldn't get beyond a certain place as long as I kept it to myself.

Opening my heart in confidence with another brother in the Lord became a God-

ordained strength for me.   Whenever I
would feel weak, I knew there was some-
body there I could talk with and pray with.
And even when I would succumb to the
temptation, I would share that with my
prayer partner and not allow the Adversary
the old place of dominion in my life by
keeping it between me and God only.

There is also the feeling of not wanting
to have to confess the same old sin to my
prayer partner again, so I often withstand
the temptation based on that. It's not that
he would have any negative thoughts toward me, but I want to behave
accountably—I don't want to have to always keep mentioning old things!!

Brother, there is victory when you partner with another brother or brothers. It's
powerful to learn to trust one another, and
grow in strength with one another as you
walk together with them and with Jesus—in
integrity of heart.

Lessons Regarding
Sexual Temptation
*As a film director, this brother was hired
to make a motion picture about the people
and culture of France for a popular theme
park. Sexual temptation was something he
least expected to encounter while doing this
family entertainment project.*

I was working on a film which required significant location scouting, which meant that before I ever shot any film, I had to go on extensive tours of the cities and country-sides of France—the real "star" of the film. This film required the full cooperation of the French Government, so as I embarked on this 5-week tour of France, my personal escort was a French Government official, who turned out to be a very beautiful woman. This was a big problem because my attraction to this woman was immediate, and I would have to work closely with her in order to make this multi-million dollar project happen.

Before I proceed, let me point out the strengths and weaknesses I carried with me into this situation.

Strengths:

• I rarely have problems with lust;

• I was raised in a godly home so the concept of sexual purity was deeply ingrained in me throughout childhood (I was a virgin until my wedding night);

• I'm happily married to a woman I find extremely attractive;

• I'm determined to never let the Lord or my wife down.

Weaknesses:

• At that time, my wife had just given birth to our first child . . . and as many men know, that's a season of abstinence which can enhance one's vulnerability.

• This was my first trip overseas. Nobody over there knew me. I was totally separated from accountability.

• I was rising fast in my career. This can produce an euphoric and foolish feeling of power that sometimes makes you feel like all "the rules" don't apply to you.

• This woman—my key government contact—to whom I was strongly attracted, was *also* attracted to me.

Added to all of these liabilities was the fact that this woman and I were touring the most romantic country on earth. It was "first class" all the way with chauffeurs, the best hotels of Europe, four-star restaurants—just like a $100,000 dream vacation.

During this whole time she made verbal invitations toward me. She would continually reserve adjoining hotel rooms with one thin door separating the two rooms. To say the least, it was important for me to stay in touch with my wife by phone during this trip.

One night, as part of our scouting circuit, we were sitting in a restaurant in a romantic port village. The hotel was just upstairs. After dinner this woman hit me with a direct proposition. I responded as I did to all the other advances she'd made before: I again simply affirmed with a smile, "I just can't. I'm a happily married man." I strove to be diplomatic, but direct.

That night in my hotel room, I experienced tremendous inner conflict. Here I was, a Bible-believing Christian, absolutely committed to serving the Lord in purity, madly in love with my wife, yet I was shocked at how overwhelming the force of temptation was. While praying earnestly to God for help, it occurred to me to confront myself in the mirror. I looked into my own eyes and said out loud all the reasons why it would be absolutely wrong and disastrous to commit adultery. I took out a picture of my wife. And into the mirror, I reaffirmed my love for her and the scriptural truth of walking in obedience to God.

So that evening, as well as throughout the entire trip, I escaped the clutches of disaster. I'm happy to say that we didn't even touch beyond our first handshake.

I should also point out that the old adage about cold showers is accurate. They work. I took several during the trip.

Here's what I learned through the entire experience:

(1) Regardless of how great our holy zeal may be or how strong our Christian upbringing was, we all have "fallen flesh" that

is extremely vulnerable to temptation.

(2) Never play with infatuation. The early stages of temptation are fun. It is such an ego-boost to have a woman be "interested" in you. But don't even think about flirting, i.e., getting too friendly.

(3) Avoid tempting situations. Now that I've been through that experience in France, I've been more careful than ever. In recent years I've had to interview potential secretaries for my business. On two occasions, I had a very frustrating time finding anyone qualified for our unique demands. Yet, on both occasions, the only women perfect for the job were particularly good looking and a bit "forward." So I felt it would be best to keep searching for qualification without potential temptation.

(4) Be accountable. On my French tour I tried to be accountable to a non-Christian associate, but he said, "Gosh, I hope you won't regret passing on this great opportunity!" (Thanks, buddy!)

That 5-week French tour came in two segments. So before the second segment began, I went back home to the States and was able to tell my Christian friend about the temptation I would be facing during the remaining three weeks. I told him that when I returned from the trip, he needed to ask me how well I did in resisting temptation. I asked him to "grill me." Knowing that I would be coming home to that interrogation really helped, in addition to diligent prayer, and—when the temptation reached dangerous levels—affirming to myself in the mirror the Truth of God's Word and the folly of sin.

Chapter Six:
Men Learning Integrity in Relationships

Integrity with My Wife

A seminar speaker on tax law and who has an income tax practice.

Last year my wife and I were at a point where we needed to "tighten the belt" on our finances. I told her that we needed to stop any unnecessary spending for several months. She and I agreed that we would both postpone buying any "extras" for ourselves until our finances were in better shape.

One week after telling her this, I went with a friend to a special garage sale—one that featured baseball cards. This is an area of great interest to me because I have made significant investments in the baseball card market. (If a person knows what he's doing and is patient, it can be quite a lucrative instrument of investment.) At this sale I found a rare rookie card which I've wanted to purchase for quite some time. Not only that, but the seller had *two* of them and he made me a deal I *couldn't* refuse. I went to the bank and withdrew the money needed to buy the cards. It was such a *great* deal—I just *knew* my wife would understand!

When I arrived at home, my wife asked me, "completely out of the blue," if I had purchased any baseball cards. Suddenly, I remembered our agreement that neither one was to make any extra purchases that were not absolutely necessary. Caught with her question hanging in the air, I quickly changed the subject so I could avoid admitting that I had transgressed our agreement.

As soon as I dodged the issue, I knew that I had crossed a line in the spiritual realm. Truth and deceit are very spiritual issues. I knew that if I didn't confess the fact that I had transgressed our agreement, it would be the first time in our relationship that I had ever lied to her.

But wait, did I *tell* my wife a lie? Had I *uttered words* of deceit?

No!

I had avoided an answer and was "scot-free," I was tempted to argue to myself!

But I had deceived her by withholding information that was tightly hinged to a mutual agreement. I was ducking into the shadows, avoiding the light of exposure. And that's a lie. I knew if I allowed deceit to enter our relationship now, our marriage would never be the same. *I* would never be the same. I would carry that sin around with me and it would cast a shadow on every area of my life: my marriage, my career, and my leadership at church. That's why sin is like leprosy—it spreads . . . until we confess it and repent.

I knew the Lord wanted me to get this issue dealt with fast. So I went to my wife and explained what had happened. Although I was willing to resell those coveted cards, my wife didn't feel I should. It was actually a relief for her to see my commitment to "keeping a clean slate" in our marriage. If I had confessed my sin to the Lord, and promised to not repeat the offense, but had not been willing to be accountable to my wife by admitting my willful transgression, not only would my integrity as a husband have suffered, but I would have allowed a small issue to become a wedge between me and my best friend—my wife.

I've never regretted telling the truth to this day . . . not even if it hurts, not even if it meant that I might have to resell a 1968 Nolan Ryan rookie card!

Surprised by Idolatry

A student, currently pursuing his undergraduate studies with a goal of eventual pastoral ministry.

It was late in the summer of 1988 and she was no longer displaying around her neck the small diamond pendant which I had given her for her birthday.

This was not a good sign.

Ever since I had given it to her, that pendant had been the barometer of our relationship's health—or lack of it. When our relationship was "on," the pendant was on her neck; when we were "off," the pendant was off. Two weeks after it had come off her neck, she broke up with me for the third and "final" time.

I went into my prayer closet—literally kneeling over my shoes and hunched under my shirts—and cried. It was the only place in the apartment where the neighbors wouldn't hear me wailing before the Lord. With tears streaming down my face, I brought my case before the throne of God.

"What happened? God, you promised!"

And I waited.

Nothing.

"How could You let her become so callous?" I cried again. "I committed my life to her with no compromise! I was determined that she would become everything Christ wanted her to be. I was committed to work with You in that process! God, she means *everything* to me! *I live for her*! She's supposed to become my wife! Lord, I love only her. I *idolize* her . . . ! I . . . *IDOL*!!??"

It was at this point in my prayer that the

realization struck. Something had gotten way out of alignment. I became quiet in my closet. I finally heard the Father's voice. He reminded me of my first love: Jesus.

What had happened to me was that my eyes had become so fixed on God's *promise* that I lost sight of *God*, the Giver of all good promises. My original commitment to this woman was good. It started out in right alignment for I sought "that I might sanctify and cleanse her with the washing of water by the word" (Ephesians 5:26). I had once said to her, "You may break up with me, you may end up hating me, but I am committed to your growth in Christ."

However, as I felt her slipping away, my response was to clamor and compromise in an attempt to preserve the relationship. That's where my priorities got jumbled. Like Abraham, I clamored for an Ishmael. Like Esau, I had sold my birthright. And the more I clamored, the more contempt she displayed toward me until the necklace came off the "final" time.

But God came down into my prayer closet where I wept in repentance. He met me there and restored my soul. And once my priorities were straightened out and Jesus was once again the first-love of my life, God was then free to work mightily and redemptively in my circumstances.

I praise God for showing me how the integrity—the *totality*—of my heart had been compromised. For having repented and re-prioritized, things were restored.

I thank the Lord that today that woman and I are serving the Lord together, and this November she and I will celebrate our fourth wedding anniversary, as we are expecting a baby to be added to our home.

Relationship with
Spiritual Leadership

A consultant to young CEOs in the area of path finding, strategic analysis, and repositioning.

Leadership is not a foreign virtue in the realm of my profession. In fact, I've dealt with leaders and leadership consistently in my line of work. However, within the first year of having been made a deacon in my church, the spiritual side of leadership gave rise to a number of new questions I hadn't before confronted.

On one hand, I wanted to be submissive and loyal to church leadership. Most of us know that to be an effective leader you need to be properly submitted to the authority over you. But on the other hand, I had strong convictions about certain aspects of direction that our church leadership was taking. There were a couple of issues I was uncomfortable with. While I wanted to continue being a church deacon, I also knew I had to express certain points of view that might not be popular with the pastor.

However, an interesting battle was going on inside of me. It was like a voice was saying, "Just keep your mouth shut! You're a deacon, and you've finally gained a certain amount of respect, so don't blow it or you'll lose it all! Maybe someday, if you hang in there, you'll be in a position to change how things are done."

In conflict with this voice, was another Voice: the Voice I now know was the Holy Spirit. It seemed to me Jesus was impressing these convictions upon my heart. It was as if He were saying: "I didn't make you a deacon so you could sit by quietly and give up your own points of view in order to protect your church position. What would be the purpose of My putting you in a church position, only for you to pretend to be someone other than who I made you to be? I want you to submit your viewpoint to leadership. Don't be afraid to be the 'real you.' That's the only kind of deacon I can use. Be prepared to resign if they find your views aren't representative and supportive to the direction of the church."

So, I sent a letter to my pastor telling him my views and offering my resignation if he felt my views were not representative of the type of leadership our church required. He then asked if I wanted to discuss my opinions. I agreed to meet with him and he later spent several hours answering my questions. During our conversation, God gently showed me how much I didn't know about what was going on at the church and why things were being done the way they were. I was humbled.

After coming to a greater understanding of our church's focus and the purpose for their mode of operation, I withdrew my resignation. And later, I became more involved than ever in building ministry within the church. Had I buried my convictions or just become cynical and unsubmissive, I would not have been able to move into more authority in God's plan. Leadership in ministry grew out of lining up my beliefs with my actions and walking in the responsibility in which God had placed me. It involved integrity of heart toward (1) my convictions, (2) the Lord's corrections, and (3) my deeper call to committed service.

Expressing conflicting convictions to people, especially people in authority, isn't comfortable for any of us. And to express our opinions does not mean we are necessarily being rebellious or unsubmissive. It's all in the motivation of the heart and the spirit in which it is shared.

True submission is also uncomfortable at times.

It was ironic that as I submitted to God and expressed myself, my pastor took me seriously enough to submit himself to me! This had a profound impact on my understanding of God's authority and how God wants us to follow willingly, and learn the true spirit of servant-leadership. He desires to remove any impediments to our unbelief or obedience. But that removal must start with a recognition and dealing before God with the conflict in our hearts. By obeying God's leading to speak, although it was difficult, I understood the deacon role and responsibility at a deeper level. Although the truth seemed to hurt at first, in reality it healed.

Chapter Seven:
Integrity of Heart—
In Front of Jesus

For over twenty years I have been privileged to be the invited guest of conference after conference where either hundreds or thousands of pastors would gather for edification and inspiration toward ministry. It is safe to say that I've ministered to a half-million pastors in one way or another—having travelled to over 20 nations, and time and again across the United States, not to mention via cassettes, radio, and television.

I refer to this fact, not as a point of pretension or pride, but because it might help you, dear brother, grasp the number of times I have been asked a certain question. It is phrased in many ways, but the essence of the inquiry is a desire to know a "secret" or a "key" to effective life and growth as a servant-leader under Jesus Christ.

Many want to know the number of hours I pray daily—the number of hours I read the Word—the number of hours per week I prepare sermons—the number of personal calls I make on people. . .Always, always, always, the question is—"How MUCH DO YOU DO to assure God's blessing on your life?"

It's the human mistake we all are inclined toward. It's based on the idea that the achievement of *some* quantity of *something* is a guarantee of success, whatever a person's life goal or vocation.

But my answer has always been the same; pointing to the fact that the *only quantity* God is really interested in as far as our lives are concerned is that *our whole heart* be His.

The subject of this small book has focused on the matter of "integrity of heart," noting that true integrity—by definition—involves the whole, the complete, the entire, the undiminished, the unfragmented, the totality of our heart being opened *to* Father God, shapeable *by* the Holy Spirit, and growing *in* Jesus Christ.

To conclude, I want to relate a story which I think may summarize *how* such a walk with the Lord may be perpetuated.

I Was About Eleven Years Old

When I was a boy, I was early introduced to a means my mother would use in dealing with each of us children—my brother, my sister, and me. Whenever Mama thought any of us might be tempted to be less than truthful because of the pressure of a situation where possible correction may follow an honest confession, she would take a precautionary step.

Instead of simply asking, "Did you do (such and such). . .?"; she would precede the question with a statement. This statement had a very sobering effect on me, because it so vividly evidenced the reality of my accountability to be truthful in the eyes of God. Mama would say, "I'm going to ask you a difficult question, Jack. But before I do, I want to say, I'm asking it 'in front of Jesus.' "

She wasn't playing games.

She wasn't threatening.

She wasn't using a religious ploy.

Rather, in our house we took the Lord seriously. Our home was a happy place to live, but we really believed in the genuine things about God's love, His kindness, His blessing, His salvation in Christ, and the beautiful truth of His Word. And when Mama would say, "In front of Jesus," a powerful image would come to my mind.

We all knew God is everywhere, all the time. But there was a unique sense of the immediacy of the Living Lord when those words were spoken. I could imagine Jesus seated on a throne immediately to my left as I stood face-to-face with my mother and prepared to hear whatever question she had.

A Visit to Dicky's House

I had come home from a friend's house one afternoon, having been most of the morning at Dicky's—a kid a few months older than I who lived across the street. We played together a great deal of the time, so there was no reason for anything unusual to be thought when I, an 11-year old boy, came home that day.

But I discovered the next morning as I

was about to leave for school, that my mother had "felt" something about my return home that day.

I had just finished my breakfast and was about to leave the kitchen and get my school things so I could head out. But I was stopped before I left the room, when my mother turned from the kitchen sink, and while drying her hands said, "Jack—I want you to wait a minute. I need to talk with you."

Her voice had that tone which children recognize of their parents when the issue is sobering and the consequences might be undesirable. I stood there, nervously waiting for what she was going to say.

"Son, when you came home from Dicky's yesterday, I had a very strange feeling go through me." She paused, thoughtfully. "At first, I didn't know what to do about it; then, I prayed last night, and I believe the Lord showed me simply to do what I'm doing right now."

"Jack, I want to ask you what happened at Dicky's house yesterday. And I'm asking this—*in front of Jesus.*"

I was frozen to the floor. The moment was one of those crystalline ones which seems as though it could be shattered by a whisper. On the one hand, I *knew* what happened at Dicky's house and knew I didn't want anyone else to know. And on the other hand—there to my left—the Throne of my Living Savior, Jesus Christ, was as real to me as though I were in heaven itself.

I began slowly. . .awkwardly. . .guiltily.

"Well, Mama," I said rather quietly and with hesitation. "When I was at Dicky's, after we'd been playing in the living room for a long time, he said to me, 'C'mon into my room a minute.'

"When he said that, he kinda laughed, and looked around to see if his mom or dad were anywhere they could hear. Right then I felt something bad was about to happen, but I went with him anyway.

"When we got in his room, he closed the door and then opened one of the drawers in the chest there. He reached way back and brought out a little tiny telescope."

I hesitated all the more, feeling the embarrassment of the confession I was about to make.

"But Mama, it wasn't a telescope." I paused again. Waiting. Not wanting to go on. "Instead, Mama, when you looked into it, there was. . .a naked woman." My eyes were moist. I looked into the face of my mother, feeling ashamed.

"What did you do, Son?" she inquired.

"We laughed," I admitted.

"How did you feel then?"

"Mama," I said with sincerity, "I felt bad."

" Then, Son. What do you want to do now?"

I walked toward my mother, whose arms opened to me as I did, as I said, "I want to pray, Mama."

And we did.

And although that event took place over four decades ago, at its root is a truth that has always continued to be just as alive and present today as it was then. *I am living my life in front of Jesus.*

I'll never know how many things that morning's confrontation and confession may have saved me from in my yet-to-be-realized future as a teenager and young man. Just as surely as I don't really know "how many" of anything I do or have done may have contributed to some degree of fruitfulness in my life and ministry, as others have asked me to quantify human efforts.

But I do know this.

I know that there are no limits to what God can do *in* a life, what He can do *through* a life, and what He can grow *around* and *within* a life, when it's lived—*in front of Jesus.*

That's the place where integrity of heart will always be sustained. For our consciousness will be on Him, not on things. And with Jesus in view, all life, fruitfulness, and fulfillment are certain to be realized with time—however tempting or trying the path.

Let's live our lives out that way.

In front of Jesus.

DEVOTIONS

IN THE FIRST EPISTLE TO
TIMOTHY

Contributed by Bob Anderson

With this epistle, the Apostle Paul was seeking to encourage Timothy, a young pastor, as he led the congregation at Ephesus through a number of difficult problems. Timothy had a significant amount of work cut out for him: false teaching needed to be effectively fought with the Truth; church leaders needed to be chosen with wisdom; different social classes in the church required extra sensitivity; and church worship needed to be brought into order. All of this was to be accomplished while maintaining an exemplary life, accurately teaching the apostolic faith!

This epistle has not only served as a universal handbook for pastors and leaders throughout the ages, but it is a particularly relevant book for any man pursuing deeper spiritual maturity.

(It is suggested that this devotional be used for stimulating discussion and prayer within a small group of men meeting regularly.)

☐ **Today's Text:** 1 Timothy 1:1-4 *(key v. 3)*

1 **Today's Truth:** Paul's first order of business was to charge Timothy to confront false teachers—an issue Paul had previously discussed with him. In addition to the spreading of erroneous doctrine that mixed law with grace, there were those who expanded Old Testament genealogies, making up names that didn't exist and stories to go with them.

Today's Thoughts: _____

_____

_____

☐ **Today's Text:** 1 Timothy 1:5-7 *(key v. 5)*

2 **Today's Truth:** For those who love "bottom-line" conclusions, verse five is a treasure. God's commandment doesn't stimulate debate or the wrestling with words as human philosophies do. Rather, it produces within people an unhypocritical faith, a conscience free of guilt, and a heart that flows with pure love.

Today's Thoughts: _____

_____

_____

☐ **Today's Text:** 1 Timothy 1:8-11 *(key v. 8)*

3 **Today's Truth:** The law is designed to instruct the ignorant and to judge the ungodly, not to condemn those who walk with Christ in faith.

Today's Thoughts: _____

_____

_____

☐ **Today's Text: 1 Timothy 1:12-14** *(key v. 14)*

4 **Today's Truth:** Paul describes the Lord's grace as "exceedingly abundant." The Greek phrase is very strong, conveying the idea that the grace of God "super-abounded" toward Paul.

Today's Thoughts: _____

_____

_____

☐ **Today's Text: 1 Timothy 1:15-17** *(key v. 16)*

5 **Today's Truth:** At times, we are all woefully aware of our own unworthiness and sinful depravity. But Jesus provided a "showcase" of grace in Paul, "the chiefest of sinners," so that we may take heart. None of us is out of God's reach to save. (cf. Isaiah 50:2a)

Today's Thoughts: _____

_____

_____

☐ **Today's Text: 1 Timothy 1:18-20** *(key v. 18)*

6 **Today's Truth:** It's interesting that Paul's charge to Timothy to "wage the good warfare" was predicated upon "prophecies previously made" concerning him. In order to fight effectively, we need to be confident of God's personal direction for us.

Today's Thoughts: _____

_____

_____

☐ **Today's Text:** 1 Timothy 2:1-4 *(key v. 1)*

7 **Today's Truth:** Paul's words are challenging yet very comforting at the same time. Regardless of who sits on human thrones, there is One to Whom we can bring our government in prayer and see dramatic results. Because all earthly thrones exist in the shadow of His, we can pray with confidence.

Today's Thoughts: _____

_____

_____

☐ **Today's Text:** 1 Timothy 2:5-7 *(key v. 5)*

8 **Today's Truth:** Jesus is the ultimate Mediator between man and God because He is both. We do not come to a "representative" of God, we come to God in human form—the Son of Man.

Today's Thoughts: _____

_____

_____

☐ **Today's Text:** 1 Timothy 2:8-10 *(key v. 8)*

9 **Today's Truth:** The physical expression of up-raised hands can be a difficult step for someone new to this pattern of worship. It cuts deep into human pride, and by its very posture acknowledges human surrender and dependence upon God. But that's what makes it so powerful! When our worship is lifted *up* in such childlike openness, that's when God sends *down* His power!

Today's Thoughts: _____

_____

_____

☐ **Today's Text:** 1 Timothy 2:11-15 *(key v. 11)*

10 **Today's Truth:** This verse is not a prohibition of women speaking in church, but rather has to do with quietness of demeanor; a call to not being "mouthy," pushy, brash, or haranguing.

Today's Thoughts: ————————————

————————————————————————

————————————————————————

☐ **Today's Text:** 1 Timothy 3:1-7 *(key v.3)*

11 **Today's Truth:** A key word describing a man who "rules his own house well" is *gentle*. The Greek word conveys someone who is "fair, reasonable, and considerate," not legalistic or harsh.

Today's Thoughts: ————————————

————————————————————————

————————————————————————

☐ **Today's Text:** 1 Timothy 3:8-11 *(key v. 11)*

12 **Today's Truth:** When Paul says the wife of a spiritual leader is to be *reverent*, the Greek conveys that she is to be "worthy of respect"—a decent and honorable person—just as husbands are also to be *reverent* in their demeanor.

Today's Thoughts: ————————————

————————————————————————

————————————————————————

☐ **Today's Text: 1 Timothy 3:12-16** *(key v. 16)*

13 **Today's Truth:** When Paul proclaims "great is
the mystery of godliness," he's not saying, "Boy,
who could EVER understand this?" The word
mystery in the New Testament means "something once hidden which is now revealed." It's
"great" in its *significance and power*, not in its
obscurity.

Today's Thoughts: _____

_____

_____

☐ **Today's Text: 1 Timothy 4:1-5** *(key v.1)*

14 **Today's Truth:** Nobody begins their faith-walk
intending to fall away. And nobody who walks in
faith with Jesus needs to walk in tormenting fear of
eventually falling away someday. As long as we
live in submission to those in spiritual authority
over us and we're accountable to one another, we
have a great safeguard against backsliding.

Today's Thoughts: _____

_____

_____

☐ **Today's Text: 1 Timothy 4:6-8** *(key v. 8)*

15 **Today's Truth:** Paul's not rejecting the virtues of
physical exercise. He's putting it all in perspective:
godliness is forever, affecting our entire being.

Today's Thoughts: _____

_____

_____

☐ **Today's Text:** 1 Timothy 4:9-11 *(key v. 10)*

16 **Today's Truth:** Why do we give the Lord our personal best, hard work, and we keep on serving Him even in the face of tribulation? Because, Paul says, "we trust in the living God" who is the Savior of everyone who will believe!

Today's Thoughts: _____

_____

_____

☐ **Today's Text:** 1 Timothy 4:12-14 *(key v. 14)*

17 **Today's Truth:** We've all had desires to be more gifted like this person or that. But God has placed in each of us a unique giftedness (Eph. 4:7-8) for a special destiny nobody else has (Jer. 29:11). Our job is to simply receive His gifts and use them.

Today's Thoughts: _____

_____

_____

☐ **Today's Text:** 1 Timothy 4:15-16 *(key v. 15)*

18 **Today's Truth:** Do you want to be a success? "Meditate on these things . . ." In Joshua 1:18 the Lord promises that if we meditate on God's Word and obey it all, then we will be prosperous and have good success. 1 Tim. 4:15 also urges that we give ourselves totally to what God has spoken.

Today's Thoughts: _____

_____

_____

☐ **Today's Text: 1 Timothy 5:1-4** *(key v. 2)*

19 **Today's Truth:** We are to regard "younger women as sisters, with all purity." So much of what determines whether we are tempted or not towards the opposite sex is our mindset. If we learn to see Christian women as sisters and non-Christian women as souls in need of Jesus, the potential for sexual lust rapidly dissipates.

Today's Thoughts: _____

_____

_____

☐ **Today's Text: 1 Timothy 5:5-8** *(key v.8)*

20 **Today's Truth:** Someone who does not provide for his own family has not only ignored the basic principles of the Christian faith, he's transgressed the common sense held by most non-Christians.

Today's Thoughts: _____

_____

_____

☐ **Today's Text: 1 Timothy 5:9-12** *(key v. 10)*

21 **Today's Truth:** For a widow to receive financial support from the church, she must have a reputation for good works and must have had a faithful marriage.

Today's Thoughts: _____

_____

_____

☐ **Today's Text: 1 Timothy 5:13-16** *(key v. 14)*

22 **Today's Truth:** Though this verse is given in respect to young widows, the caution is universally valuable: that we "give no opportunity to the adversary to speak reproachfully." Since he is the "accuser of the brethren"—and a diligent one at that—we should avoid *all* appearance of evil.

Today's Thoughts: _____

_____

_____

☐ **Today's Text: 1 Timothy 17-20** *(key v. 20)*

23 **Today's Truth:** The public correction of leaders who are in public ministry, occasioned by the failure of integrity, is not an act of cruelty. The goal is to cleanse the wound in the Body of Christ, instill godly fear in other leaders so they won't fall, and help the congregation learn about the tragedy, together at one time, rather than allow rumors to distort the truth and harm "the sheep."

Today's Thoughts: _____

_____

_____

☐ **Today's Text: 1 Timothy 5:21-23** *(key v. 22)*

24 **Today's Truth:** Paul warns against haste in the appointing of elders. Choosing leaders with solid integrity is a crucial responsibility.

Today's Thoughts: _____

_____

_____

☐ **Today's Text: 1 Timothy 5:24-25** *(key v. 25)*

25 **Today's Truth:** So much of our labor for the Gospel which nobody presently sees will one day be open before all eyes. That's not what motivates us to serve, of course, but it can greatly comfort us in seasons when we feel unappreciated or at times when we see little harvest for so much sowing.

Today's Thoughts: —————————————

—————————————————————————

—————————————————————————

☐ **Today's Text: 1 Timothy 6:1-2** *(key v.1)*

26 **Today's Truth:** Christian slaves serving unbelieving masters were to do so with honor and thereby be effective witnesses. Although none of us serve as slaves, we do serve bosses—some not easy to respect. Yet we're to "work as unto Christ."

Today's Thoughts: —————————————

—————————————————————————

—————————————————————————

☐ **Today's Text: 1 Timothy 6:3-6** *(key vv. 5, 6)*

27 **Today's Truth:** Any person who views godliness as a means to selfish gain will be fruitless and disappointed. But if the equation is turned around where godliness and God's kingdom is sought first, God's blessing and provision will abundantly follow (cf. Mt. 6:33, John 10:10, Ps. 16:11).

Today's Thoughts: —————————————

—————————————————————————

—————————————————————————

☐ **Today's Text: 1 Timothy 6:7-10** *(key v. 10)*

28 **Today's Truth:** Who doesn't enjoy financial prosperity? Let's admit it! Is it fair to say it's "nice?" But what's the *real* issue here? If we maintain a relationship with Jesus in which He is our first love and top priority, other issues in life will tend to find their proper place. God gives us the power to enjoy what we have (Ecc. 5:19), but if money is priority one, sin and sorrow will result.

Today's Thoughts: ———————————
_____
_____

☐ **Today's Text: 1 Timothy 6:11-12** *(key v. 12)*

29 **Today's Truth:** "Fight the good fight of faith!" Having faith in this world is not without conflict, but we are assured ultimate victory: "Many are the afflictions of the righteous, but the Lord delivers him out of them all" (Psalm 34:19).

Today's Thoughts: ———————————
_____
_____

☐ **Today's Text: 1 Timothy 6:13-16** *(key v. 16)*

30 **Today's Truth:** Jesus dwells in "unapproachable light." No wonder our countenances are changed when we spend time with Him and our integrity is renewed in His Presence! (cf. Psalms 17:15 & 34:5)

Today's Thoughts: ———————————
_____
_____

☐ **Today's Text: 1 Timothy 6:17-21** *(key v. 20)*

31 **Today's Truth:** Paul's final charge to Timothy, and hence to us, is that we should guard the Gospel as a rare treasure, making sure that our message is clear, pure, and without the pollution of human philosophies.

Today's Thoughts: _____

_____

_____

Additional Resources for Biblical Manhood

Available from Jack Hayford and
Living Way Ministries

AUDIO CASSETTE MINI-ALBUMS (2 tapes)

Honest to God	SC122	$8
Redeeming Relationships for Men & Women	SC177	$8
Why Sex Sins Are Worse Than Others	SC179	$8
How God Uses Men	SC223	$8
A Father's Approval	SC225	$8
Resisting the Devil	SC231	$8
How to Recession-Proof Your Home	SC369	$8
Safe Sex!	SC448	$8
The Leader Jesus Trusts	SC461	$8

AUDIO CASSETTE ALBUMS (# of tapes)

Cleansed for the Master's Use (3)	SC377	$13
Becoming God's Man (4)	SC457	$17
Fixing Family Fractures (4)	SC217	$17
The Power of Blessing (4)	SC395	$17
Men's Seminars 1990-91 (10)	MSEM	$42
Premarital Series (12)	PM02	$50
A Family Encyclopedia (24)	SC233	$99

VHS VIDEO ALBUMS

Why Sex Sins Are Worse Than Others	WSSV	$19
Divorce and the People of God	DIVV	$19
Earthly Search for a Heavenly Father	ESFV	$19

Add 15% for shipping and handling.
California residents add 8.25% sales tax.
Request your free Resource Catalog.
Living Way Ministries Resources
14820 Sherman Way • Van Nuys, CA 91405-2233
(818) 779-8480 or (800) 776-8180